DOLPHINS

BY GEORGE SHEA
PICTURES BY ANNE MARSHALL RUNYON

EMC PUBLISHING ST. PAUL, MINNESOTA

Library of Congress Cataloging in Publication Data

Shea, George.
  Dolphins.

  Includes index
  SUMMARY: Examines fact and fiction about dolphins, emphasizing their friendliness toward and interaction with humans.
  1. Dolphins—Juvenile literature. [1. Dolphins] I. Runyon, Anne Marshall. II. Title, III. Series.
  QL737.C432S53   599.5'3   80-18259
  ISBN 0-88436-770-3

Copyright 1981 by EMC Corporation
All rights reserved. Published 1981.

No part of this publication can be adapted,
reproduced, stored in a retrieval
system, or transmitted in any form
or by any means; electronic, mechanical
photocopying, recording, or otherwise,
without the permission of the publisher.

Published by EMC Publishing
180 East Sixth Street
St. Paul, Minnesota 55101
Printed in the United States of America
0 9 8 7 6 5 4 3 2 1

EMC SCIENCE READERS

ALLIGATORS
BATS
BEARS
BIG CATS
DOLPHINS
SNAKES
SPIDERS
WHALES
WOLVES

A woman falls from a tall ship in the middle of the night. No one sees her or hears her cries for help.

She starts to swim this way and that in the darkness. She has no idea which way is land and safety. The shore may be many miles away.

Then, suddenly, in the water, a dark shape appears next to her. A shark! She swerves in terror, moving off to the right. Suddenly, the shape moves up and touches her left hip. She sees that it is not a shark, but a friendly dolphin. The dolphin continues to guide the woman to the right. There, she finds the sea calmer and easier to swim in. Then, the animal gets behind and to the right of her in the water. It stays with her until the water is no longer deep and her feet touch bottom. Finally, the woman stands up and walks onto dry land. She turns and sees the dolphin zip happily away back into the depths of the sea.

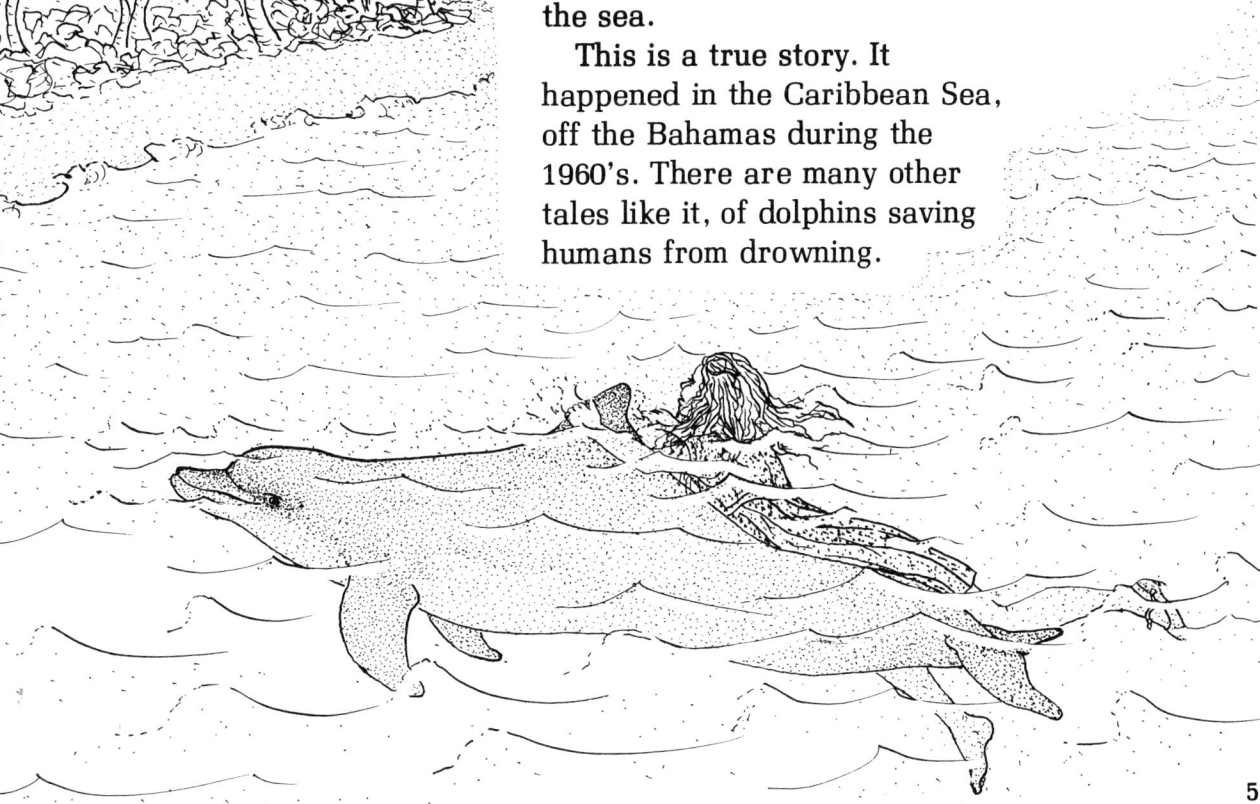

This is a true story. It happened in the Caribbean Sea, off the Bahamas during the 1960's. There are many other tales like it, of dolphins saving humans from drowning.

THE STORY OF PELORUS JACK

Dolphins seem to love people and the ships people sail in. Often, when they see a ship coming, they like to leap out of the water to greet it.

Sailors are very fond of dolphins too. Usually, they are very careful not to hurt them. They consider it very bad luck to kill a dolphin.

About a hundred years ago, there was a narrow passage of water off the coast of New Zealand. It was called French Pass. Sailors used it as a shortcut, but it was a very dangerous one. Its waters were very tricky and its bottom was filled with jagged rocks.

One stormy morning, a ship called *Brindle* started to go through the passage. Suddenly, a blue-gray dolphin popped its head out of the water. It began jumping up in front of the ship as if to welcome it.

The dolphin started to lead the way through the dangerous channel and the ship followed it. Finally, the ship arrived safely on the other side. The happy sailors aboard the *Brindle* felt the dolphin had helped them. They called the friendly, useful dolphin "Pelorus Jack."

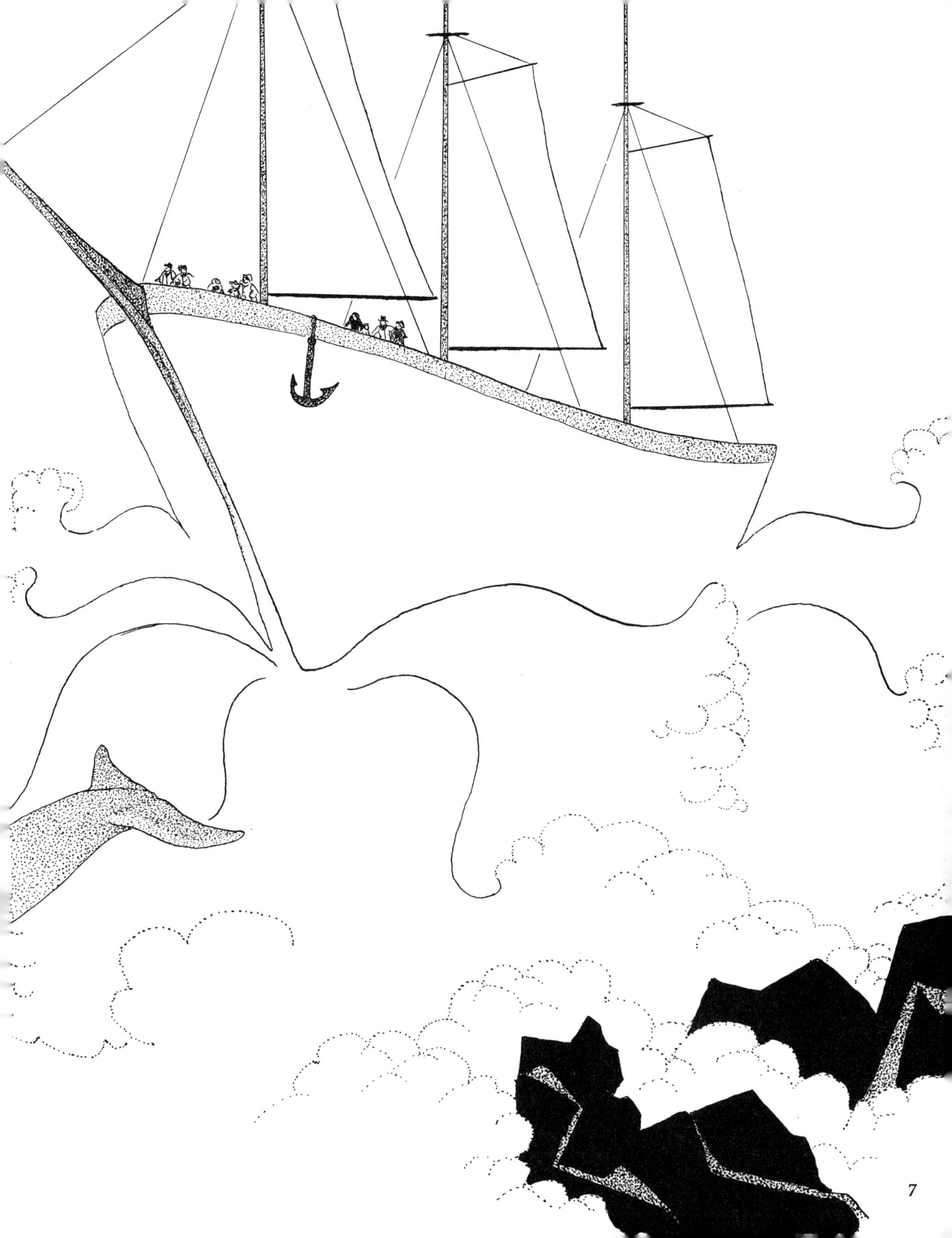

Pelorus - an instrument like a ship's compass. It is used to help guide ships at sea.

After that, for over 30 years, Jack showed up and led every large ship that came along through the passage. Every sailor on every ship came to know "Jack" by sight. And they all trusted him to lead them through the waters of French Pass.

Then, one day in 1903, a drunken passenger aboard a ship called the *Penguin*, fired a shot at Jack. The bullet struck the dolphin, and he disappeared below the water. The crew of the ship wanted to lynch the man who had shot Jack. Only the ship's captain saved his life.

But Jack was gone. Everyone feared that he was dead. Then, suddenly, two weeks later, he showed up again. The famous dolphin seemed to be all right. And, at once, he went back to his job of helping every large ship that came along through the difficult channel.

That is, he helped every ship but one. Jack never turned up to help the *Penguin* again. One day, several years later, the *Penguin* was wrecked in the passage and sunk.

In 1912, 41 years after he was first sighted, Jack disappeared. The helpful dolphin was never seen again.

THE DOLPHINS STRIKE BACK

Twice every year, in November and March, thousands of dolphins swim past the Japanese island of Iki.

In March of 1980, several American newspapers carried the following story.

Japanese fishermen on the island of Iki decided that the dolphins were eating too many of the fish they were trying to catch. So they trapped a thousand of the dolphins with huge nets. The next day, the fishermen took knives and spears and killed five hundred of the trapped dolphins.

That night, an American named Dexter Cate sneaked in and opened up the nets. About half the trapped dolphins got away and swam out of the nets into the open sea. Cate was caught by Japanese police and put in jail.

But the next day, when the fishermen started to take their boats to sea, they couldn't believe their eyes. Four thousand dolphins had gathered in the waters around the harbor. The dolphins blocked the harbor and kept the fishermen's boats from going out to sea!

Why did the dolphins do what they did? No one knows for sure. But probably they were hoping to somehow save their friends and relatives who were trapped in the nets.

There are thousands of dolphin stories. Some tell of the dolphin's unusual intelligence. Some tell of its great playfulness. (Dolphins love to play with people for hours at a time. There are many stories of dolphins giving people rides on their backs.)

There are many stories, too, of dolphins helping each other. Some U.S. Navy personnel reported seeing the following happen: Once, a dolphin was knocked unconscious by an underwater explosion. It couldn't come to the surface to breathe. (Dolphins must come to the surface every six minutes to breathe.) Suddenly, other dolphins came and placed their bodies under their injured friend. They raised its body up to the surface so that it could breathe. They stayed with it until it was well enough to take care of itself.

A Section of the Minoan Dolphin Fresco, Palace of Knossos, Crete

THE HUMANS OF THE SEA

Human beings have always been fascinated by the dolphin. It is thought to be one of the most intelligent, playful, friendly, and gentle of creatures.

Thousands of years ago, the ancient Greeks had a legend about the dolphin. They believed that once upon a time, dolphins were human. For one reason or another, the gods had sent them to live in the sea. The Greek poet Homer tells the following story: The Greek god Dionysus was kidnapped by pirates. But he so frightened the pirate crew with his feats of magic that they threw themselves overboard and were at once turned into dolphins.

The tale caused the poet Ossian to write: "Diviner than the dolphin is nothing yet created, for indeed they were aforetime men, and lived in cities . . ."

Nowadays, no one really believes that dolphins were ever human. But some scientists believe that dolphins may be as intelligent and perhaps even more intelligent than people!

Many scientists don't agree. Many say that, right now, there's just no way of telling.

But what about the dolphins? What *do* we know about their intelligence?

THE DOLPHIN'S BRAIN

Scientists consider brain size to be a good way of measuring intelligence. Humans do not have the largest brains. Three kinds of animals have brains larger than those of humans: whales, elephants, and dolphins.

Large whales have brains about six times the size of humans. One scientist, Dr. John C. Lilly, believes the great sperm whale to be a creature of great intelligence, perhaps more intelligent than any human.

But this cannot really be proven. For one thing, there is no way of measuring the intelligence of the great whales. These great creatures spend most of their lives under water. Also, because of their great size and appetites, it has been next to impossible to study these creatures closely. The average sperm whale grows up to 60 feet (18 meters) in length, and eats a ton of food a day. So far, it has not been possible to keep a large whale for study purposes in a zoo or aquarium.

And elephants . . .?

The brain of an elephant is about four times the size of the human brain. We believe elephants to be among the most

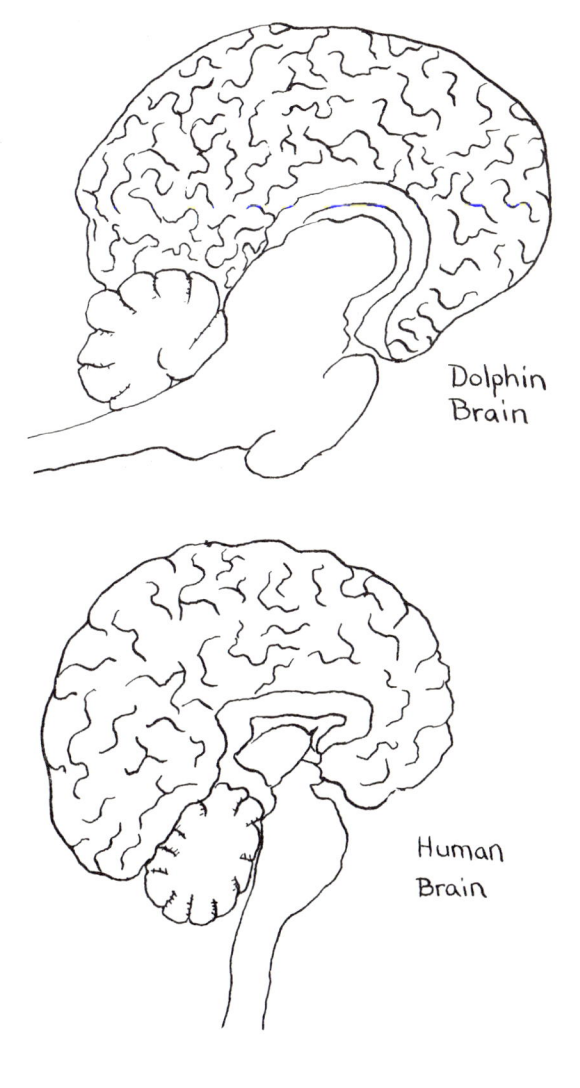

Dolphin Brain

Human Brain

intelligent of land animals. But, so far, no serious efforts have been made to study their intelligence.

And what about dolphins . . .?

The brain of the bottle-nosed dolphin (the most intelligent of all dolphins) weighs about 1700 grams. The brain of the average human weighs only about 1450 grams. And so, the brain of the dolphin is about 20% or one-fifth larger than that of a human being.

A dolphin's brain seems to be different from ours. For one thing, it is *wider*. Why is this so?

We do know that different parts of the human brain have different uses. One part of our brain is used to *think* with, to reason things out. Another part helps us to *see*. Another part helps us to *taste*. And so on.

But the dolphin lives in a different world than we do. It spends most of its life under water. For one thing, it has to find its way around under water. Sometimes it travels thousands of miles in search of food.

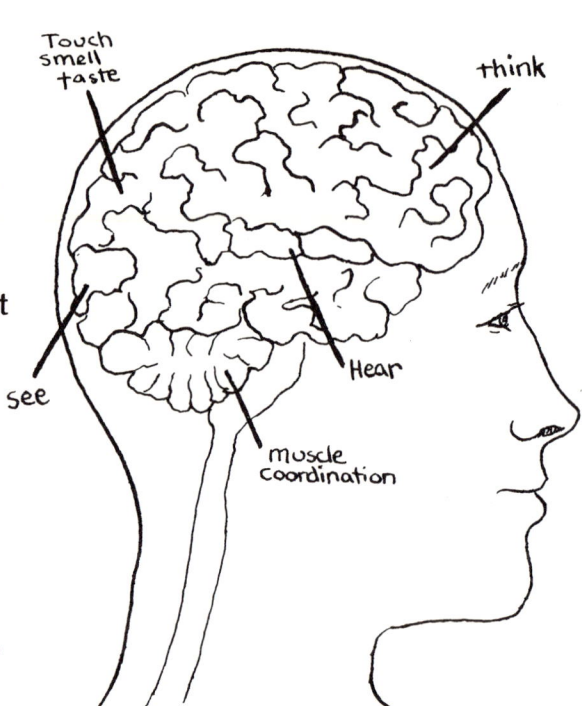

Human Brain

And so its brain has to perform different tasks from ours. For example, a great deal of the dolphin's brain is taken up with *hearing*. Dolphins use their hearing to help them get around. (We'll say more about this later in the book). This explains why its brain is wider.

Another question is often asked. If dolphins are so smart, then why don't they write books and invent things as humans do?

The answer may be simple enough. Dolphins live in the sea. They don't live on land as we do. They don't have hands as we do. And so they can't write or build things as humans do. (They do have flippers which they use to help them steer around the ocean). But it's just very possible that dolphins have no *need* of books or computers or other great inventions. Their lives in the sea work perfectly well without such things.

Scientists list several reasons why they believe dolphins to have unusual intelligence:

- They seem to be able to measure and work out tough math problems underwater.

  For example, they must come up to the surface to breathe at least once every six minutes. At the same time, they must often dive hundreds of feet, chasing after food. What this means is that the dolphin has to constantly figure its distance from the surface and the time needed to reach air again. It must work out these problems based on its speed.

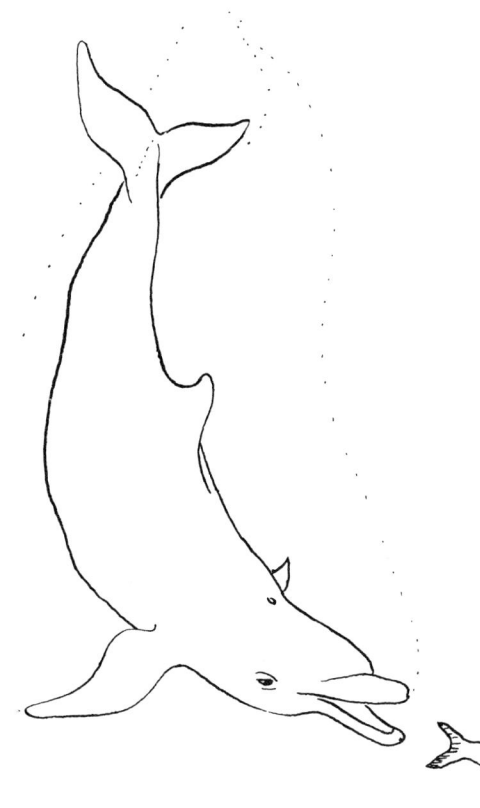

This is no simple matter. All animals do certain things by *instinct*, a natural ability that has nothing to do with intelligence. For example, a cat licks or cleans itself by instinct. But some scientists believe that the dolphin's ability to figure distance and time goes well beyond mere instinct.

In any math class, then, a dolphin would be sure to come out with straight "A' "s.

- Dolphins learn quickly. Dolphins in aquariums and in other learning situations, often easily learn how to perform tasks taught them by humans.
- They are very curious.
- They not only learn games quickly, they invent new games of their own.
- They show that they care for others and quickly understand other's situations.

For example, when they play with humans, they are very careful not to hurt them. Dolphins love to play by grabbing people's legs and arms in their mouths. Dolphins are very strong and have long rows of sharp teeth. They could easily do a lot of damage, but they take care never to seriously hurt anyone. They seem to know just how far they can go when playing around humans.

So what *is* the answer—?
- ☐ Dolphins are more intelligent than humans.
- ☐ They are much less intelligent.
- ☐ Their intelligence is of a very different type from ours.

The only answer we can safely give is the last one. To be sure, the intelligence of dolphins is of a very different kind from ours. As for *how* intelligent they are, no one knows for sure. Scientists are still studying these wonderful creatures. Very probably, they will have a more complete answer in the future.

For now, probably, the best and most complete answer of all is a combination of all three possibilities:
- ☑ Yes, dolphins are more intelligent than humans (in some ways).
- ☑ Yes, they are much less intelligent (in some other ways).
- ☑ Yes, their intelligence is certainly of a very different type from ours.

Later, we'll have more to say about dolphin intelligence. For example, we'll try to answer such questions as: Can dolphins and people really talk to each other?

But, first, let's answer some other questions about dolphins—questions such as . . .

WHERE DO DOLPHINS COME FROM?

Believe it or not, they come from the land. Millions of years ago, dolphins lived on land as we today.

They were little creatures, about a foot high. They were flat footed, four-legged and hairy, with large snouts and tails. They looked somewhat as dogs do today. We believe they may have lived in the trees.

human

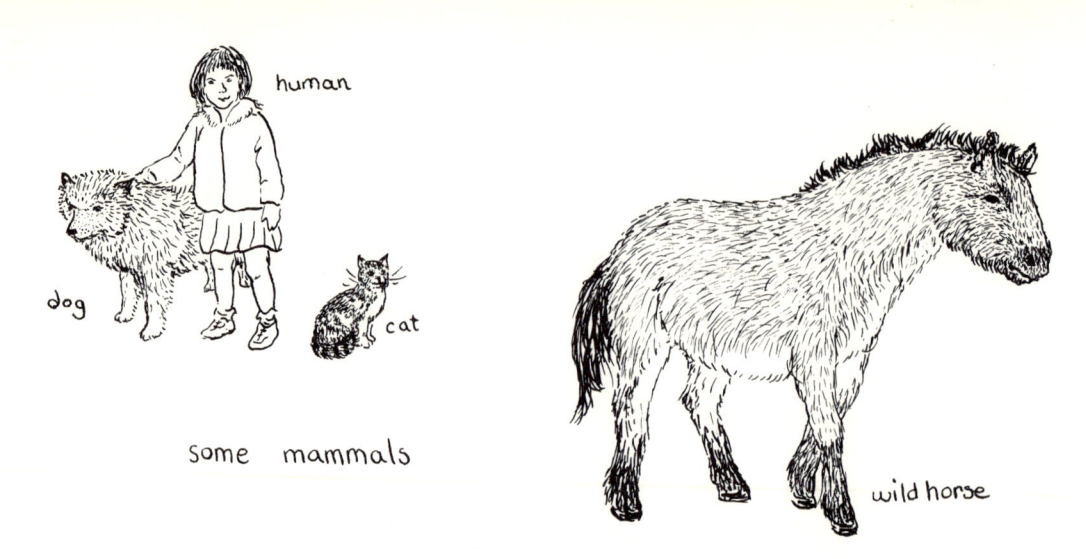

dog cat

some mammals

wild horse

Anyway, they were among the first *mammals*. They didn't lay eggs as other creatures did. But they gave birth to live young who nursed on milk from their bodies. Their babies stayed with their mothers for a time and learned from them.

This ability to learn was something new among the animals of the earth. In the course of time, the mammal's ability to learn made it the master of the planet Earth.

We humans of today are mammals, like most of the land animals we are familiar with.

Scientists believe this early ancestor of the dolphin (called the *creodont*) was a *carnivore* or meat eater. But there is evidence, too, that suggests it may have been a *herbivore* (or plant eater).

creodont → → → → → → → →

16

About 125 million years ago, the little furry creodont decided it wasn't too happy with life on land. Perhaps its small size made it easy prey for larger animals. And so it gradually began to move toward the sea. At first, it probably just went down to the shore and scooped fish out of the water with one of its paws. Also it found that it could plunge into the water to escape from its enemies.

As the creodont began to spend more and more time in the sea and less on land, its body began to change. Little by little, it lost its fur. This was replaced by an underskin of blubber for protection against the cold. Its little hind legs began to shrink into its body, and its front legs took the shape of flippers.

THE BODY OF THE DOLPHIN

It took millions of years, but gradually its body became more and more streamlined like that of a fish. Its ears shrank back into its body to become just tiny holes in the sides of its head. Its eyes moved back to each side of its head which, bit by bit, became longer and longer. Its nostrils became a single blowhole at the top of its head. This made it easier to breathe while floating.

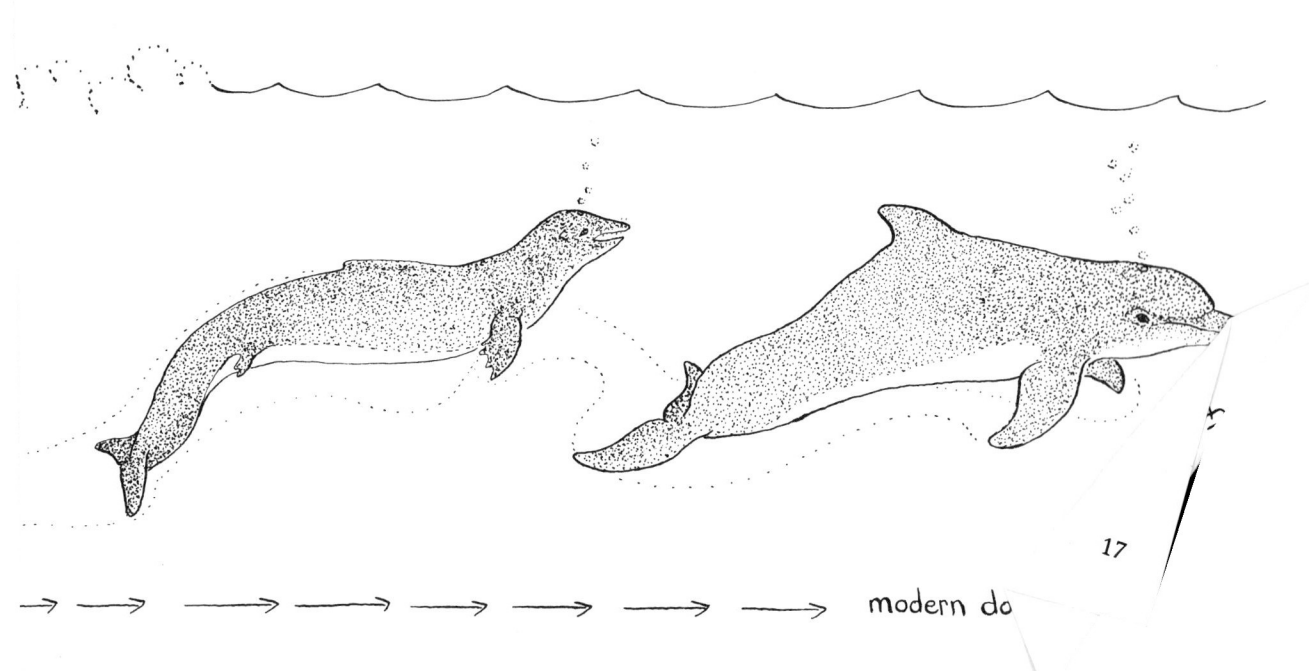

modern do

In time, its body became perfectly suited to life in the sea. Today, the dolphin's body is better suited to life in the sea than our bodies are to life on land. The dolphin uses less energy making a fifteen foot leap in the air than a human would use climbing a ladder to hang a picture.

The dolphin moves through the sea with the greatest of ease. As a matter of fact, the sea water *holds up* the dolphin's body. Dolphins, like whales, couldn't weigh nearly as much as they did if they lived on land.

Here we see a diagram of the body of a bottle-nosed dolphin. Most of its body parts are easy to see.

1 *Jaws and Teeth.* The dolphin's long beak contains two very powerful jaws with from 80 to 100 very sharp teeth. The teeth of young dolphins are very sharp, while those of older dolphins are somewhat worn down.

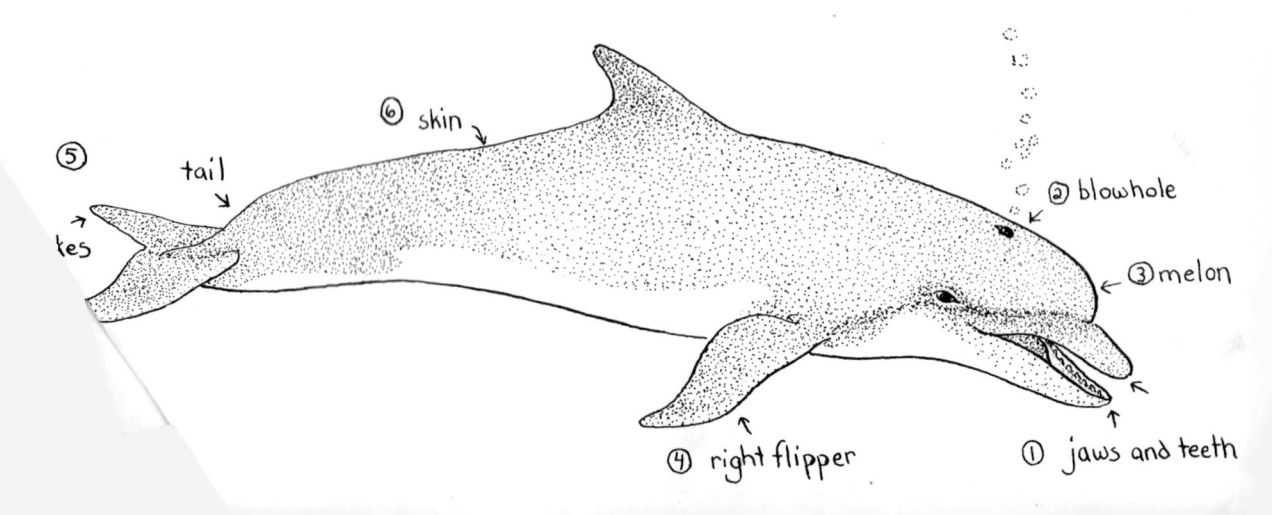

2. *Blowhole.* This is what the dolphin uses to breathe with. Every six minutes or so, the dolphin must rise to the surface of the water to take a breath. When it does, it opens its blowhole and sucks in air. This calls for split second timing.

As the dolphin leaps clear of the water in a perfect curve, it opens its blowhole to take in new air and let out old.

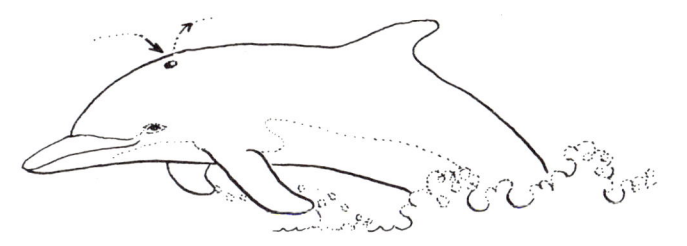

3. The dolphin's *forehead* or "melon" is very large and made up of oily and fatty substances. Many people make the mistake of thinking that this is where the animal's large brain is stored. But the actual brain is further back.

Why is the dolphin's forehead or "melon" so large? Perhaps it is that way so that it can protect the brain. Some believe that the dolphin uses it as a sort of radar scanner for picking up sounds in the water. (We'll explain more about this later).

4. The *flippers* do not push the dolphin through the water. They are used for balance and steering.

5. The dolphin uses its *tail* and the two lateral (sideways) *flukes* at the end of it to move itself around.
The dolphin's tail flukes can whip the water so powerfully that the animal can stand or scoot across the water on its tail.

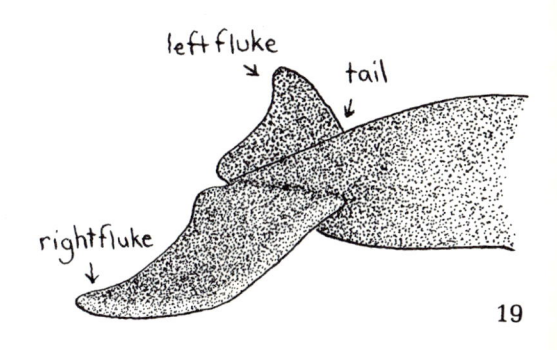

6   The dolphin's *skin* seems rubbery and hard to the touch. But, actually, it's easily damaged. It's the only thing that makes dolphins afraid of contact with humans. Before they will let a person get too close, they must be sure that there is nothing in the human touch that might hurt their skin.

THE DOLPHIN'S SENSES

Dolphins see well in both air and water but only if their eyes stay moist. If a dolphin stays out of the water too long, the wetness on its eyeballs dries up and the animal becomes temporarily blind.

As far as we know, dolphins have no sense of *smell*. But they do have a strong sense of *taste*. Just as land animals track their prey by smell, it's believed that dolphins can track down a fish in the water just by the taste it leaves.

HOW A DOLPHIN HEARS

The U.S. Navy has been studying the hearing of dolphins for years. So far, it hasn't figured out exactly how they can hear so well underwater. The Navy would like to find out, simply because the dolphin's built-in sonar hearing system is ten times better than anything the Navy—with its billions of dollars—has been able to produce.

The way dolphins hear is something like an underwater device called *sonar*. This is how it seems to work: as a dolphin swims underwater, it sends out a series of *clicks*. The clicks bounce off an object underwater and bounce back to the dolphin's brain. Suddenly, the dolphin knows everything about the object: its distance, its direction, speed, size, and shape.

It can also tell about its *substance*. Tests have been made in which dolphins were blindfolded with special eye shields. They could tell the difference between objects that looked exactly the same but were made of different metals. In other tests, they have been able to tell the difference between things made of wood and cloth and other kinds of materials.

Dolphins see fairly well, though not as well as we do. Often, the water under the seas is very clouded. A human diver has trouble seeing anything more than a hundred feet away.

But, with its built-in sonar, the dolphin can tell about things that go on underwater miles away. It knows that far ahead a dangerous shark is cruising; it knows that, not so far away, a school of small, tasty fish may be found. Also, about a mile off, and off to the right is a long slender ship made of metal, moving at high speed underwater: a submarine.

In other words, with the help of its built-in sonar, the dolphin knows a very great deal about the world in which it travels. To be sure, it knows much more about *its* world than we do about ours.

Think about this: Suppose you were blindfolded and asked to walk down a dark, empty street. Suppose that, half a mile away, another person were coming toward you.

If you had anything like the dolphin's built-in sonar, you could tell:
- how far away the other person was
- in what direction they were going
- how fast they were going
- how big they were

Also, you'd have a rough idea of what they looked like.

DIFFERENT KINDS OF DOLPHINS

Up to now, we've been talking about dolphins as though there were just one kind of dolphin in the world—the bottle-nose.

This is the dolphin that humans know best. The bottle-nose is the one we most often see doing tricks in aquariums and marine parks. A bottle-nose known as "Flipper" was the hero of a popular television show some years ago.

But there are lots of other kinds of dolphins. Here are some examples:

KILLER WHALE
The largest of the dolphins. Grows up to 30 feet (9 meters) long. Although it is called a "whale", it is really just a large dolphin.

PILOT WHALE
Up to 22 feet (7 meters) long. Pilot whales travel around together in groups or *schools* of hundreds. They're found in the Atlantic, Pacific, and Indian Oceans. Like the killer whale, the pilot whale is really a large dolphin.

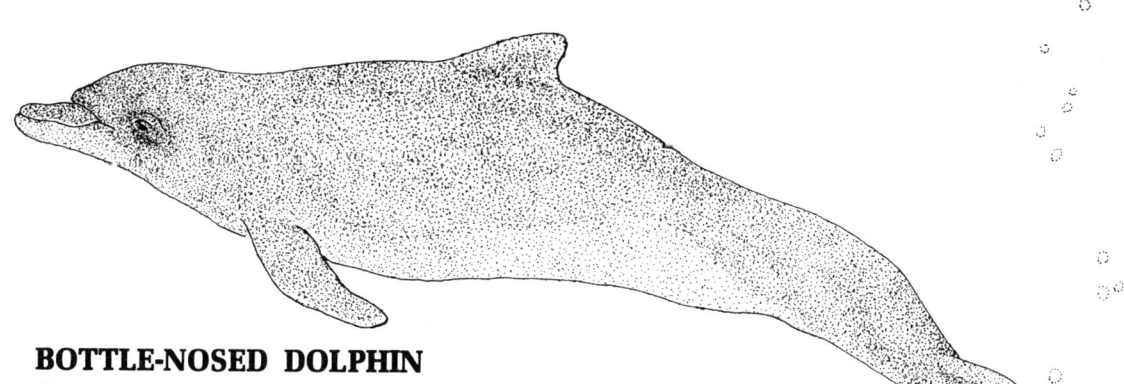

BOTTLE-NOSED DOLPHIN
Grows up to 12 feet (3.7 meters) in length. The biggest of them weigh as much as 800 pounds.
The very popular bottle-nose is found in the North Atlantic, also the Baltic, Mediterranean, and the Black Sea.

RISSO'S DOLPHIN
Pelorus Jack (who used to guide the ships through the channel) was a Risso's Dolphin. It's found in all seas, but stays away from cold water regions.

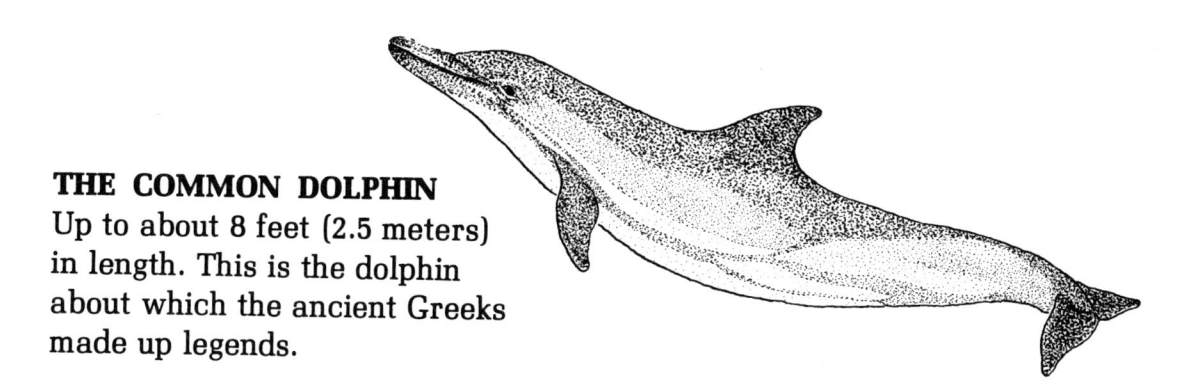

THE COMMON DOLPHIN
Up to about 8 feet (2.5 meters) in length. This is the dolphin about which the ancient Greeks made up legends.

WHITE BEAKED DOLPHIN
WHITE SIDED DOLPHIN
Both these species grow to about 9 feet (2.8 meters) in length. They are found in the North Atlantic in large groups or schools.

ROUGH TOOTHED DOLPHIN is known for its rough teeth. It has about two dozen in each jaw. It lives in tropical and warm seas around the world, but it is seldom captured.

SPOTTED DOLPHIN

is found in the coastal waters of the western Atlantic.

PORPOISES AND DOLPHINS—WHAT'S THE DIFFERENCE?

There isn't very much. Porpoises tend to be smaller than dolphins. Also, they have a less snoutlike beak. Actually, people often use the words "dolphin" and "porpoise" to mean the same animal.

Porpoises and dolphins are both *cetaceans* or members of the whale family. They belong to the *odontoceti* or toothed whales. This is why some kinds of dolphins have the word "whale" in their names.

Again, it is important to remember that the killer whale and the pilot whale, though they are called "whales," are really just "big" dolphins. The same may be said of the beluga and the narwhal, two small toothed whales found in Arctic seas. They are also considered to be dolphins.

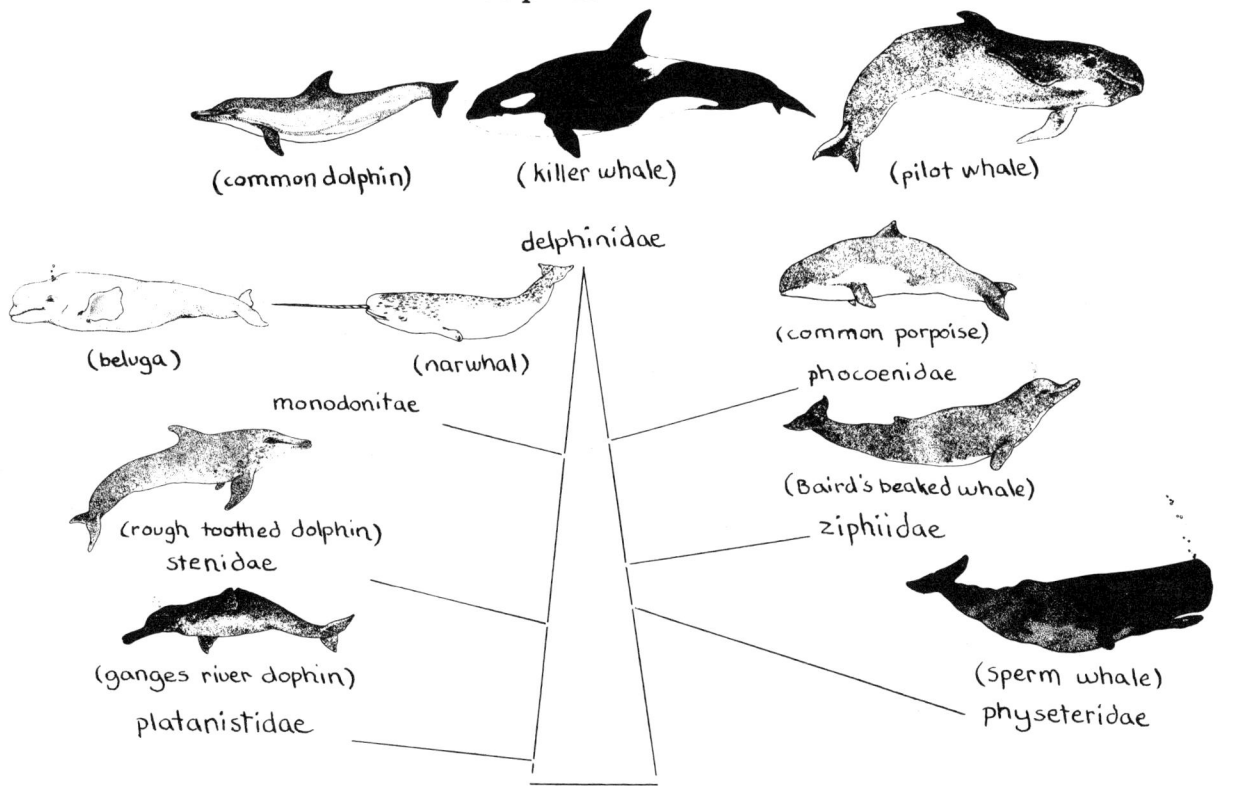

(common dolphin)
(killer whale)
(pilot whale)
delphinidae
(beluga)
(narwhal)
monodonitae
(common porpoise)
phocoenidae
(rough toothed dolphin)
stenidae
(Baird's beaked whale)
ziphiidae
(ganges river dolphin)
platanistidae
(sperm whale)
physeteridae

KILLER WHALE!

People think of dolphins as friendly and gentle creatures. But the killer whale is a large dolphin that is one of the fiercest killers that lives in the sea.

Killer whales are highly intelligent. They attack like wolves in well organized packs. They attack and kill dolphins, sharks, and sometimes large grey and blue whales.

Until 1965, everything that swam in the sea lived in fear of the killer whale. And that included people. "Beware the tiger of the sea" was a common saying.

TAMING THE KILLER WHALE

Then in 1965 something happened that changed everything. A Canadian sculptor was asked to make a statue of a killer whale. The sculptor didn't have a killer whale to model for him. So he set out to kill one and use its body as a model.

He was able to harpoon a killer whale. But, as the animal lay wounded in the water, he couldn't bring himself to finish it off.

Instead, he brought it back to the aquarium in Vancouver, British Columbia. He gave it some medicine and nursed it back to health. To everyone's surprise, he and the animal became great friends.

It wasn't long before other aquariums began to capture and tame killer whales. The killer whales turned out to be very fond of people and quite intelligent.

A killer whale named Namu liked to give people rides on its back. It lived at the Seattle Aquarium.

Before long, some scientists came to believe that the killer whale is even more intelligent than the bottle-nosed dolphin. In *The Whale, Mighty Monarch of the Sea*, undersea writer and explorer, Jacques Cousteau writes:

According to everyone who has worked with both killer whales and dolphins—including experts from the U.S. Navy—the (killer) whale is much more intelligent than the dolphin. They understand and learn twice as fast as their smaller cousins.

MOST DOLPHINS ARE NEVER LONELY

Ocean-going dolphins and other toothed whales are, it seems, never really alone. Not a great deal is known about their life at sea. They do, after all, spend most of their lives underwater. And that makes it hard to study them. But it is believed that they zip around the oceans in groups. The groups range in size from a thousand or more to smaller subgroups of perhaps 20. (The Pacific spotted dolphin travels in huge herds of several thousand. They must look like a small traveling city at sea.)

Life is different for freshwater or river dolphins. They tend to be much less social. They live in small groups and are sometimes almost alone.

Do dolphins travel around a great deal at sea? Three scientists placed tags on 47 captured bottle-noses off the coast of Florida. They kept track of each dolphin's movements. They found that the dolphins moved about in an area of about 85 square kilometers. This is an area about the size of the city of Washington, D.C.

Like every human society, every dolphin group has its rules. For one thing, they do not fight over food. When a herd of dolphins tracks down a school of fish, the members of the herd surround the school. Then each dolphin takes its turn picking out a fish and moving off with it to let another have its turn.

What do they eat? Dolphins eat a great deal of fish. Food at sea is generally plentiful, and in its lifetime, the dolphin eats a great deal of butterfish, anchovies, mullet, herring, and baby squid.

There does seem to be a certain amount of *dominance* among dolphins.

Dominance: when one animal in a group has power or control over one or more animals in the group.

spotted dolphins

Dominance is also common among many land animals such as wolves, dogs, and chickens.

A group of seven captive dolphins was closely studied. (Groups of five or six dolphins are always seen traveling around together, even as part of a larger group.)

The largest male in the group seemed able to threaten the females and the smaller males in the group. He did this by showing his teeth or lunging at them with his snout. He did these things just to show them who was boss.

The leader of any dolphin group is believed to be always the strongest male. When dolphins travel, females and their young are kept in the middle of the herd. Males tend to travel on the outside of the group to protect the others. A dolphin mother will sometimes move to the outside to protect its young in time of danger.

WHEN DOLPHINS MATE

Unlike many other animals, dolphins mate all year round. Studies by scientists seem to show that they are not monogamous.

Monogamous: a situation in which an animal or a person has only one mate.

Female dolphins seem to be more monogamous than males. In other words, they seem more likely to have only one mate. But male dolphins usually mate with more than one female.

It is quite something to watch a male and female dolphin courting each other. First, the male picks out the female he wants to mate with and, for four to six weeks, they flirt with each other. They stroke each other with their flippers, nuzzle each other with their beaks, and stroke each other with their bodies. From time to time, the male will try to impress the female by jumping in the air and other stunts. Or he will quickly dash at her while she will pretend to get away. At other times, they may dance together in a very graceful water ballet.

Finally, their mating is completed, and the female becomes pregnant. Her pregnancy is a long one. Dolphin mothers take a full twelve months for their babies to develop inside their bodies. (Human mothers are pregnant for only nine months.)

THE BIRTH OF A DOLPHIN

Finally, the baby dolphin is ready to be born . . .

Dolphins, unlike most mammals, are born tail first instead of head first. The baby dolphin looks just like its mother. It is fully formed, and able to see, hear, and swim. It is 3 feet (.9 meter) long and weighs from 25 to 30 pounds (55 to 66 kilograms).

The first few moments of its life can be tricky. The young dolphin must quickly rise to the surface to take its first breath. If it doesn't, it will drown.

Its mother helps it in this, nudging it gently up to the surface. Once it takes its first breath of air, however, the little dolphin is far from on its own. Its mother looks very closely after it, staying with it all the time.

As a matter of fact, baby dolphins may be said to have more than one mother. Before the baby's birth, its mother chooses another female dolphin to act as a sort of "aunt" for the new dolphin. Together, mother and aunt swim with the baby dolphin between them. If it starts to wander away, they nudge it quickly back where it belongs.

The young dolphin gets milk from its mother's breast, like all mammals do. After six months or so, the baby may eat solid food, usually a piece of fish offered by its mother. But it is a full eighteen months before the young dolphin goes off to feed on its own.

Dolphins are not fully grown up until they are six years old. (No one is exactly sure how long dolphins live. But 40 years seems to be a good guess.)

Luckily for the life span of dolphins young and old, there are few other creatures in the sea that put it in any danger. It has few enemies. The killer whale is the toughest and most feared. Sharks sometimes attack dolphins. But a dolphin is often a good match for a shark. (They kill sharks by ramming their bodies with their beaks.)

But in recent years, as is sadly the case with so many animals, the greatest danger to the dolphin has come from human beings.

THE DOLPHIN AND THE TUNA INDUSTRY

American Pacific tuna fleet fishermen first began killing large numbers of dolphins in the 1960's.

Why? It was because some species of dolphins often traveled with yellowfin tuna. Even now, no one knows just why the dolphins swim with the tuna. But they do.

Until the 1960's, fishermen had caught tuna one at a time. But then, the fishermen found a way to use the dolphins to help them catch larger numbers of tuna. They developed a new method of tuna fishing called "purse-seining."

It works like this. Dolphins swim close to the surface of the water. The yellowfin tuna swim just below them. When a fishing boat spots a herd of dolphins in the water, it knows that the tuna will be swimming right below them.

Speedboats go out and herd the dolphins together. Then the tuna boat puts out a long metal seine or net that fences in the dolphins and tuna. The net is closed shut at the bottom to keep the tuna from getting away.

Finally, the net is pulled in by the boat in such a way that it gets lower at the far edge. This gives the dolphins a way of getting out of the net and getting away.

Often, this worked out. But too often, there were accidents. The dolphins got trapped in the net. They could not climb out and get to the surface where they could breathe. Many drowned. In 1966, about 244,000 dolphins died in purse seines. During the 1960's and early 1970's, millions of dolphins were killed in purse seines. The fishermen had no use for their bodies. Their deaths were a cruel and very sad waste.

Finally, people began to demand that the killing of the dolphins be stopped. Many Americans stopped buying tuna fish as a way of showing how they felt.

Finally, in 1972, the U.S. Congress passed the Marine Mammal Protection Act. It told the tuna industry it had two years to find a way to stop killing so many dolphins. Gradually, improvements were made, and there were fewer accidents. In the year, 1978, 15,000 dolphins died in purse seine traps. This was far fewer than had been killed in earlier years. But dolphin lovers feel that the death of even one dolphin is still one death too many. They hope that, before long, the tuna industry will give up purse seining altogether.

CAN DOLPHINS AND PEOPLE TALK TO EACH OTHER?

This is a good question. A number of scientists have spent years trying to talk with dolphins.

There is no doubt that dolphins do have a language of their own. We know that they often use it at sea to warn each other of danger. The dolphin has no vocal chords to make speech as we do. Instead, it gives off different kinds of sounds from its blowhole: clicks, whistles, bleats, and creakings.

Over the years, some scientists have had success talking to dolphins by means of underwater electronic signals. One scientist was able to turn a small number of commands in English, such as "Hit the ball" and "Go through the hoop", into dolphin whistles. He broadcast the sounds underwater, and the dolphins understood them and did what they were told to do.

Other scientists have had similar successes. But so far, no scientist has been able to have a two-way conversation with a dolphin.

Perhaps no one has tried harder than Dr. John C. Lilly. Dr. Lilly began his attempts to talk with dolphins in the 1950's. By the 1960's, he was predicting that people and dolphins would be talking to one another within ten years. He built a special house in the Virgin Islands. He and his assistants lived there with dolphins 24 hours a day, seven days a week. In time, the dolphins became very friendly with the scientists.

But, by the end of it all, Dr. Lilly still could not make two-way conversation with the dolphins. He wound up returning them to their freedom in the open sea.

But, by 1979, Dr. Lilly was once again working at his dream of talking with dolphins. He was setting up another laboratory, this time in California. The lab was to be equipped with special sonar equipment and phones. With it, scientists could send out sonar signals that could be heard by dolphins swimming in the open sea.

It was hoped that, in time, the dolphins would begin to answer the signals. Then scientists would finally learn the secrets of the dolphin language.

If this happens, it could be a fascinating step forward. Some scientists, like Lilly, believe the dolphin's language is as rich and complicated as our own.

Dr. Lilly believes that dolphins may have wonderful stories and legends to tell us.

"They've been around 25 million years, with a brain size equal to and later greater than ours," he says. "I want to find out if they have sagas, teaching stories, histories. It will take a lot of work, of course, before we get to the point where they can tell us stories we can understand."

Is all this just a wild, foolish dream? Will dolphins really have much of anything to say to humans?

Who knows? But, in the meantime, the experiment certainly does seem to be worth a try. Dolphins may indeed have a great deal to teach humans. For one thing, their lives are far gentler and easier than ours. Perhaps they know something about living that we don't. Dr. Lilly has pointed out that a dolphin newspaper would carry no stories of wars or murders or other human type events.

Perhaps one day, we will pick up a human newspaper and read the following headline:

DOLPHINS TELL HUMANS
HOW TO LOVE ONE ANOTHER

Maybe this will never happen. Maybe, after all, the dolphins have nothing to say. But, in the meantime, they seem to be much better at living with one another and loving one another than we are. It would be wonderful if, by watching them and perhaps someday listening to them, we could learn how to be more loving and gentle ourselves.

INDEX

Anchovies, 29

Bahamas, 5
Beluga, 25
Blowhole, 19
Blue whales, 26
Bottle-nosed dolphin, 12, 18, 22, 23, 28
Brain functions
   dolphin, 12, 13
   human, 12
Butterfish, 29

Caribbean Sea, 5
Carnivores, 16
Cate, Dexter, 8
Cetaceans, 25
Common dolphin, 23
Cousteau, Jacques, 27
Creodont, 16, 17

Dionysus, 10
Dolphins
   as members of whale family, 25
   breathing, 9, 13, 19
   care of young, 32
   communicating, 36, 37, 38
   concern for others, 8, 9, 14, 38
   courtship, 31
   curiosity, 14
   dominance phenomenon, 29, 30
   eating habits and diet, 29
   evolution, 15, 16, 17
   friendliness to humans, 5, 6, 9, 10, 15, 26, 27, 37
   giving birth, 32
   group phenomenon, 28, 29
   habitat, 22, 23, 24
   hearing, 13, 19, 20
   hunting for food, 13
   intelligence, 9, 10, 11, 13, 14, 15, 18, 27
   legends about, 10, 23
   locomotion, 13, 18, 19
   mating, 30, 31
   parts of body, 11, 12, 13, 15, 17, 18, 19, 20
   playfulness, 9, 10, 15
   pregnancy, 31
   seeing, 20, 21
   sense of taste, 20
   skin sensitivity, 20
   strength, 15

Fishermen, Japanese, 8, 9
"Flipper", 22
Flippers, 13, 19
Flukes, 19
French Pass, New Zealand, 6, 8

Gray whales, 26
Greeks, ancient, 10, 23

Herbivores, 16
Herring, 29
Homer, 10

Iki Island, Japan, 8
Instinct in animals, 14
Intelligence
   dolphins, 10, 11, 13, 14, 15, 27
   elephants, 11
   humans, 11, 15
   whales, 11

Killer whale, 22, 26
   ferocity, 26, 32
   intelligence, 27
   kindness to humans, 26, 27

Lilly, Dr. John C., 11, 37, 38

Mammals, 16
Marine Mammal Protection Act, 34
"Melon" (forehead), 19
Mullet, 29

Namu, 27
Narwhal, 25

Odontoceti, 25
Ossian, 10

Pelorus, 8
"Pelorus Jack", 6, 8, 23
Pilot whale, 22
Porpoises, 25
Purse-seining, 33, 34, 35

Risso's dolphin, 23
River dolphins, 28
Rough-toothed dolphin, 24

Seattle Aquarium, 27
Sharks, 5, 26, 32
Sonar, 20, 21, 37
Sperm whale, 11
Spotted dolphin, 24, 28
Squid, 29

Tuna industry, 33, 34, 35

U.S. Congress, 34
U.S. Navy, 9, 20, 27

Vancouver, British Columbia, 27
Virgin Islands, 37

Whales, 11, 18, 25
   toothed, 25, 28
White beaked dolphin, 24
White sided dolphin, 24

Yellowfin tuna, 32

599.5
SHE

Shea, George.

Dolphins.

$6.95

DATE DUE	BORROWER'S NAME	ROOM NO.
MAY 29	Patrick R.	311
JAN	Shawn	37
NOV 18	R. Peterson	304
NV 22	Aaron	202

599.5
SHE

Shea, George.

Dolphins.

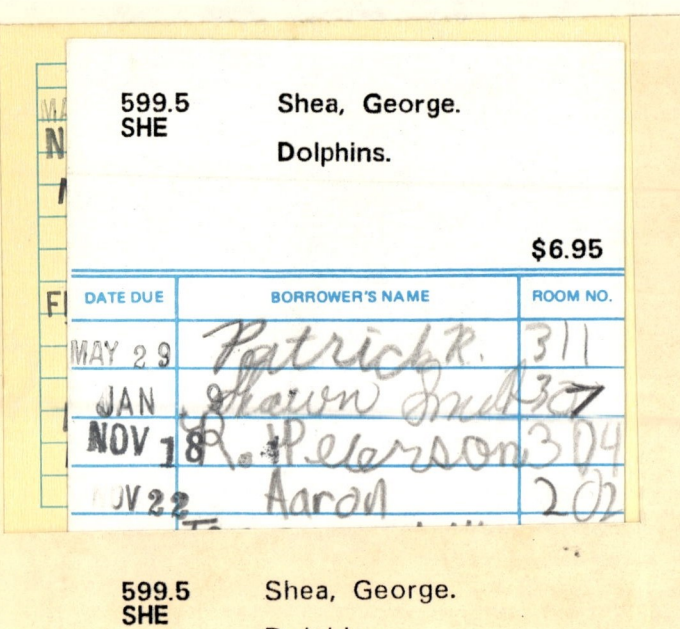

GESU SCHOOL LIBRARY
DETROIT, MI 48221

393735 015628